The Best Of
Pathways of Song

Compiled, Arranged,

Translated and Edited

by

FRANK LaFORGE

and

WILL EARHART

Volume 1 & 2 HIGH VOICE
Volume 3 & 4 HIGH VOICE *

©1934 WARNER. BROS. INC.
* ©1938 WARNER BROS. INC.

FOREWORD

The purpose of this book is to place songs of great beauty, selected from wide fields of classical and folk song literature, within reach of students. Great care has been taken to include only songs that, in the main, lie in a restricted compass. While they are worthy of the attention of the greatest artist and may well find place on the most deserving programs, they do not require elaborate technique for their effective performance.

Extreme care has been given to the translations. Effort was directed toward making them adhere closely to the original texts, both in general import and in subtleties of mood; and in the case of specific words of distinctive hue or of climactic force, occurring here and there, English words of like color or force were sought. Euphony and vocal ease were also considered in the choice of words.

In addition to the aims mentioned, the editors have sought to include in this book a goodly number of comparatively unhackneyed songs that appear to have been left to one side, quite undeservedly, by the winds of current interest. It is their hope that in this, as in the other aims, they have met with some degree of success, and have thereby promoted to some extent their cherished purpose, which is to improve and enrich the literature available to students who follow the pleasant Pathways of Song.

Frank LaForge

The name of Frank LaForge first came into world prominence as accompanist and piano soloist with Mme. Marcella Sembrich, which position he occupied for ten years. Since then he has rightfully come to be recognized as one of America's foremost accompanists and voice teachers.

Mr. LaForge's grasp of the great songs of the world is comprehensive and profound. Some conception of his knowledge of song literature may be gleaned from the fact that he has a repertoire of over five thousand memorized accompaniments embracing all schools. He has been associated as accompanist and pianist with the outstanding singers of his day, among whom may be mentioned, besides Mme. Sembrich, Mmes. Schumann-Heink, Matzenauer and Lily Pons. Among his voice pupils have been such representative American singers as Marian Anderson, Marie Powers, Lawrence Tibbett, Richard Crooks and many other operatic and concert stars.

It may be safely said that in all probability no living person knows more accurately or has studied more sympathetically the needs of the singer and particularly of the vocal student. The solutions that great artists have brought to bear upon their own problems of interpretation and vocal technique have been observed and weighted by Mr. LaForge in his New York Studio, a studio that may well be called in the true scientific use of the word, a voice laboratory.

It is upon these years of experience in studying the needs of the student singer, particularly as applied to songs that have technical as well as program value, that Mr. LaForge has drawn in compiling these books.

Will Earhart

A truly representative figure in music education, Dr. Will Earhart has been identified with every phase of music in the public schools, an unwavering influence for the elevation of musical standards and the improvement of pedagogic practices.

In addition to his work in the public schools, Dr. Earhart has been a faculty member or superintendent of innumerable summer music schools including those of Northwestern University, Columbia University, Pennsylvania State College, the University of California and Syracuse University. For many years he has been identified with the music department of Carnegie Institute of Technology.

As writer and editor he has a catalog of such length as to preclude listing here, appearing uner the imprint of representative American publishers. Specific mention, however, should be made of his *The Eloquent Baton* (a manual for conductors) and *Music to the Listening Ear*, a book for students of music appreciation. He has made many surveys and reports for the United States Bureau of Education. His contributions to musical and educational journals have been enlightening commentaries upon the history, theory, practice and social significance of music education.

He is a past president of the Music Supervisors National Conference and has been active on many committees of that organization. His services are frequently called upon as adjudicator of choral, instrumental and vocal contests.

Dr. Earhart was for many years Director of Public School Music in the city of Pittsburgh.

CONTENTS

Have You Seen But A Whyte Lillie Grow

Although the composer of this number has never been definitely determined, it is generally credited to John Dowland, an English composer (1562-1626). The poem is by Ben Jonson (1573-1637) one of the greatest English dramatists of his time and an intimate friend of William Shakespeare. Shakespeare acted in several of Ben Jonson's dramas. The poet has used the five senses to express his love.

True sincerity, simplicity of style, and a good command of pianissimo are required. If rendered in the proper manner it is one of the most effective concert songs. Unfortunately it has been modernized in several editions almost to the point of making it an insipid ballad. In this arrangement by Arnold Dolmetsch the original quaintness of the setting has been preserved.

BEN JONSON

ANONYMOUS
(1614)

Or Swans down e-ver; Or have smelt of the Bud of the Bry-er,

Or the Nard in the fire, Or have tast-ed the Bag of the Bee: O so

whyte, o so soft, o so sweet, so sweet, so sweet is shee! O so

whyte, o so soft, o so sweet, so sweet, so sweet is shee!

(pp)

Wilt Thou Thy Heart Surrender
Willst du dein Herz mir schenken

Attributed to Bach, it is now believed to have been the work of Giovannini, a violinist who lived in Berlin (1740-1782). It demands a certain charm of style and good diction.

English version by
FRANK LA FORGE

GIOVANNINI
Attributed to J.S. Bach
Setting by F. Campbell-Watson

Wilt thou thy heart sur-rend-er, So
Willst du dein Herz mir schen-ken, So

give it se-cret-ly For what we both are think-ing, None
fang es heim-lich an, Dass un-ser Bei-der Den-ken Nie-

shall the wis-er be. Our love must e'er be se-cret And
mand er-ra-ten kann. Die Lie-be muss bei Bei-den All-

Eileen Aroon

This matchless melody dates back to the early days of Irish minstrelsy, and was perhaps known in the thirteenth century. The modern version of the text reflects faithfully the spirit and intention of the old verses. As with the Scotch version of the song, *Robin Adair*, the song *Eileen Aroon* came to birth under deeply romantic circumstances.

Handel is said to have declared that he would rather have been the composer of this exquisite air than of all the music he had written. Whether or not he made so extreme a statement, the loveliness of the song is sufficient to lend color to the report. At the same time the sincere purity and simplicity of the song make it one that the humblest as well as the greatest may possess.

Old Irish Air
Accompaniment by
WILL EARHART

Text by
GERALD GRIFFIN

1. When, like the ear - ly rose, Ei - leen A - roon!
2. Is it the laugh - ing eye, Ei - leen A - roon!
3. When, like the ris - ing day, Ei - leen A - roon!

Beau - ty in child - hood blows, Ei - leen A - roon!
Is it the tim - id sigh, Ei - leen A - roon!
Love sends his ear - ly ray, Ei - leen A - roon!

When, like a di - a-dem, Buds blush a - round the stem,
Is it the ten - der tone, Soft as the stringed harp's moan?
What makes his dawn - ing glow Change-less through joy and woe?

Which is the fair - est gem? Ei - leen A - roon!
Oh, it is truth a - lone, Ei - leen A - roon! roon!
On - ly the con - stant know, Ei - leen A - roon!

4. I know a valley fair,	6. Were she no longer true,
Eileen Aroon!	Eileen Aroon!
I knew a cottage there,	What should her lover do?
Eileen Aroon!	Eileen Aroon!
Far in that valley's shade,	Fly with his broken chain
I knew a gentle maid,	Far o'er the sounding main,
Flower of a hazel glade,	Never to love again
Eileen Aroon!	Eileen Aroon!
5. Who in the song so sweet?	7. Youth must with time decay,
Eileen Aroon!	Eileen Aroon!
Who in the dance so fleet?	Beauty must fade away,
Eileen Aroon!	Eileen Aroon!
Dear were her charms to me,	Castles are sacked in war,
Dearer her laughter — free,	Chieftains are scattered far,
Dearest her constancy,	Truth is a fixed star,
Eileen Aroon!	Eileen Aroon!

★ For variety, the repeat may also be made by playing this as a chord of dotted half notes, omitting the next three notes and returning to measure three, instead of (as indicated) to measure one.

Cradle Song
Wiegenlied

It is now believed certain that Mozart did not write this song. The accompaniment is so easy that it becomes difficult. Its transparency must be preserved and the little sixteenth note passages made delicate and
even. As with all Mozartian renditions, there should be no evidence of conscious artifice.

The three final measures may be used as introduction.

Attributed to
W.A. MOZART
(1756-1791)

Original key

Good Morning

Grieg's Opus 21 consists of four songs, the texts of which are from Björnson's *Fisher Maiden*.

The whole-heartedness of Grieg is nowhere more in evidence than in this song *Good Morning*. An infectious buoyancy pervades it.

Vocally, the song requires a bright, easy and flexible tone, and, due to the rapid tempo, clear and competent articulation. The trills and mordents written by Grieg have been retained, but can be omitted by the less advanced singer without impairment of any fundamental values. It is far more important that the essential body of the song be well sung and interpreted than that these ornaments be labored over, perhaps with ill success, before basic values are secured.

BJÖRNSTJERNE BJÖRNSON
English version by
WILL EARHART

EDVARD GRIEG, Op. 21, No. 3
(1843-1907)

Serenade
Liebes Mädchen, hör' mir zu

Mr. Henry T. Finck says of this song: *"Liebes Mädchen, hör' mir zu* is as graceful and pretty as a folksong, somewhat suggestive of Schubert's *Heidenröslein."* More praise might well be given it, for the balances of melodic undulation and rhythmic movement are flawless. While the good humor of the song is infectious it is sensitive humor, never transgressing the bounds of good taste.

English translation by
WILL EARHART

JOSEPH HAYDN

1. Dear - est maid - en, hear me now,
2. When 'tis twi - light in Re - vier,
1. Lie - bes Mäd - chen, hör' mir zu,
2. Wenn es däm - mert im Re - vier,

Ope thy lat - tice hith - er. Hath my heart no
And the dark is fall - ing, Up to thee I
öff - ne leis' das Git - ter; denn mein Herz hat
A - bend - ne - bel san - ken, schwing' ich mich em -

rest, I vow, Hath no rest my zith - er.
swing me here, From the tend - rils call - ing.
kei - ne Ruh', kei - ne Ruh' die Zi - ther.
por zu dir an den Blät - ter - ran - ken.

Original key—D

Though the heav - y clois - ter wall
Then, O love - ly pen - i - tent,
Hal - ten Klo - ster - mau - ern dich
Dann, du schö - ne Dul - de - rin,

May with rig - or bind thee, Yet my song to
Bend thee down, I pray thee, And, de - spite thy
noch so streng ge - bun - den, hab - en mei - ne
neig' dich zu mir nie - der; und trotz Pfaff' und

thee will call, And, re - joic - ing, find thee.
guard's in - tent, For my songs re - pay me.
Lie - der sich doch zu dir ge - fun - den.
Pri - o - rin lohn mir mei - ne Lie - der!

I Love Thee
Ich Liebe Dich

This song was published in 1803, one year before publication of the composer's Eroica Symphony. It bore the title *Zärtliche Liebe* (Tender Love), but has been published in English under the title *Mutual Love*. As Beethoven used the text it begins with the second stanza of Herrosen's poem, *Ich liebe dich*.

A mood rarely captured by any composer other than Beethoven here finds expression. Sincerity and depth of feeling are blended with exquisite purity and simplicity. A sustained tone-line and clear diction that holds no trace of the declamatory are necessary to a right revealment of the nobility and beauty of the song.

English version by
WILL EARHART

L. van BEETHOVEN

Original key

18

If Thou Be Near
Bist du bei mir

In the notebook for Anna Magdalena Bach for the year 1725 this aria appears as a melody, with a text of unknown authorship, and with only an unfigured bass by way of accompaniment. The mood of the aria, definite as it is in a musical sense, is almost beyond description in words. Serene contemplation, an exaltation that has risen above all worldliness, are apparent. Not a religious song, but one of conjugal affection, it nevertheless interprets human relations in spiritual terms.

English version by
WILL EARHART

J. S. BACH

Original key—E♭

Panis Angelicus
Heavenly Manna

César Franck's works have been called veritable "cathedrals" in sound and this composition is no exception. A simple grandeur characterizes it and its rendition should be on broad lines with a symphonic avoidance of any rhythmic disturbance. The canonic imitation in the second verse should be well brought out. A 'cello obbligato gives color to this imitation and greatly enriches the effect of the song.

English version by
FRANK LA FORGE

CÉSAR FRANCK
(1822-1890)

Original key

grace be - yond com - pare,
gu - ris ter - mi - num.

O

O

won - d'rous
res mi -

tok - en
ra - bi - lis

of lov - ing
man - du - cat

kind - ness,
Do - mi - num,

sempre legato

sempre legato

p Need - y,
Pau - per,

cresc. low - ly,
pau - per,

f all may thy boun - ty
ser - vus et hu - mi -

share,
lis,

p Need - y,
Pau - per,

cresc. low - ly,
pau - - per,

p

cresc.

Below In The Valley
Da unten im Tale

The directness and simplicity of the typical folksong are here apparent. In a musing that holds something of the fragrance of tender memories, something of disillusionment that yet harbors no bitterness, a view of life is disclosed and withdrawn. Brahms' power to add strength and richness to the folksongs he loved, without in the slightest impairing their simplicity or otherwise altering their character, is marvelously illustrated by this accompaniment.

English version by
WILL EARHART

JOHANNES BRAHMS

Original key — E♭

3. When ten times I tell you I love on - ly
4. The_ love you have giv - en I grate - ful - ly
3. *Und_ wenn i dir's zehn - mal sag', dass i di*
4. *Für die Zeit, wo du g'liebt mi hast, dank i dir*

you___ And you will not be - lieve me, what more can I
bear,___ And I hope with an - oth - er you bet - ter may
lieb,___ und du willst nit ver - ste - hen, muss i halt wei - ter
schön,___ und i wünsch' dass dir's an - ders - wo bes - ser mag

do?
fare.
gehn.
gehn.

Amarilli

Written by one who achieved much as a singer, this song makes heavy demands on the legato and breath support. The breath marks given here add to the expressiveness of the song and it is strongly advised that they be observed.

Caccini was one of the first composers to write music for the solo voice. He belonged to the band of musicians who revolutionized music from the dramatic standpoint. This group met at the home of Bardi in Florence, Italy, which is mentioned in George Eliot's "Romola."

English version by
FRANK LA FORGE

GIULIO CACCINI
(1550-1615)
Setting by F. Campbell-Watson

Doubt can nev-er a-vail thee. Look in my bos-om and see there
du - bi-tar non ti va - le. A - pri-mi il pet - to e ve-drai

gra-ven on my heart A-ma-ril - li, A-ma-
scrit-to in co - re: A-ma-ril - li, A-ma-

ril - li, A-ma-ril - li is my loved one, A-ma-
ril - li, A-ma-ril - li è il mio a-mo - re, A-ma-

ril - li____ is my loved_____ one.
ril - li____ è il mio a-mo - - - - re.

The Bells
Les Cloches

"Les Cloches" was composed approximately in 1887, when the composer was twenty-five years of age. The original and powerful style that later distinguished his work had not then matured, but something of the poetic atmosphere, subtle and haunting, that a later technique more perfectly expressed is still to be found in this song. Debussy's selection of the Bourget poem, filled as it is with delicate half-lights, is itself significant.

The rare atmosphere requires from the singer purity and restraint of style. The voice that speaks in the poem is not that of a hearty flesh-and-blood character, but is that of a mind detached in revery so remote that only a tinge of earthly melancholy touches it. Such a mood—one often met in French works, and characteristic of Debussy—requires that the singer deliver the music instrumentally, as a flute might play it, avoiding all those dramatic, emotional emphases that in a song of another style might be imperatively needed.

PAUL BOURGET
English version by
WILL EARHART

CLAUDE ACHILLE DEBUSSY
(1862-1918)

air. / ment.

Pure, rhyth - mic and fer-vent as choir-ed
Ryth - mique et fer - vent comme une an - ti -

psal - ter, Their dis-tant ap - peal To my heart re -
en - ne, Ce loin-tain ap - pel Me re - mé - mo -

call'd white flow'rs of the al - tar, Where the pi - ous kneel.
rait la blan-cheur chré-tien - ne, Des fleurs de l'au - tel.

rit. *a tempo*

rit. e dim.

Un poco meno mosso

The
Ces

Grace Thy Fair Brow
Rend'il sereno al ciglio
(From "Sosarme"-1732)

Breadth and grandeur dwell in these classic lines. A broad tempo is to be observed. Avoid shortening such measures as the second and nineteenth of the *Largo* – being careful to give the rests their full value.

English version by
FRANK LA FORGE

G. F. HANDEL
(1685-1759)

Grace thy fair brow with con - tent - ment, Moth-er, oh! weep no more, Oh! weep no more, No! Moth-er, oh! weep no more,

Rend' il se - re - no al ci - glio, ma - dre, non pian-ger più non pian-ger più nò. ma - dre, non pian - ger

Original key

more.
più.

Grace___ thy fair brow with con - tent-ment,
Rend'___ il se - re - no al ci - glio

mf

Moth - er, oh! weep no___ more,
ma - dre, non pian - ger___ più

No, no, Moth - er,
nò nò ma - dre,

cresc.

f *p* *f*

oh! weep no more!
non pian - ger più.

p *f*

All thought of dan - ger ban - ish,
Te - mer d'al - cun pe - ri - glio.

p

Cradle Song
Wiegenlied

The collections of folksongs by Brahms, published in 1894, contain no number more appealing than this *Cradle Song.* It has appeared in many translations, not all, it must be said, of equal merit, and the Brahms accompaniment has sometimes been modified. In the version here given effort has been made to adhere closely to the German text, and the accompaniment is authentic.

English version by
WILL EARHART

JOHANNES BRAHMS

Original key

Blessed Redeemer
Liebster Herr Jesu

The first appearance of this sensitive melody was in a book by Schemelli published in 1736. It contained a large number of songs and hymns for which the melody and bass only were printed. In his preface Schemelli states that all the pieces were composed or "improved" by J.S.Bach. Musicologists since have spent much time in trying to discover which songs were composed and which simply improved by the master.

The song below, through extrinsic evidence as well as by reason of depth and sincerity of feeling and integrity of structure, appears to be certainly Bach's own composition. The necessary largeness and dignity of feeling, as distinguished from lachrymose and theatrical expression, can be secured by abstaining from sudden dynamic changes and by a broad, flowing sketching of the phrases. This is to be sung in the manner of a choral.

AUTHOR UNKNOWN
English version by
WILL EARHART

JOHANN SEBASTIAN BACH
(1685-1750)

The Jailer's Slumber Song

In this song, as in *Ah, No Stormy Wind,* the deepest emotional inheritances of a people find expression. Almost appalling is the tide of colossal feeling that mounts in the middle section. The English text clings closely, in entirety and from point to point, to the grim Russian.

Perhaps the best suggestion to the singer is that his song, as vocal melody that obeys musical demands, must not be broken, however poignant the drama that may thrust itself forward. Once complete vocal control is lost, emotion in a singer becomes ludicrous and can claim no respectful hearing. Attention to pitch and quality of tone, to attacks and releases marred by no "scoops" in pitch and no lapses from singing into speech, will safeguard the singer's delivery.

Translation from the Russian
by NINA KLIEGER
English version by
WILL EARHART

RUSSIAN FOLKSONG
Arranged by A. Borodin

Dance, Maiden, Dance
Danza, danza, fanciulla

During the lifetime of the composer none of his works appeared in print. Among his pupils were numbered Pergolesi, Piccini, and Paisiello. This song is gay and full of life. Many singers divest old songs of all their humor, thinking that they must necessarily be solemn.

English version by
FRANK LA FORGE

FRANCESCO DURANTE
(1684-1755)

45

Lied

The delicate, intangible beauty that is characteristic of Franck hovers over this song. Tragic implications are here, but no poignant outcry shatters the atmosphere of detached, mystic brooding. The artist soul of Franck was ever too suffused with beauty to be wracked by the ugly outlines of present clamoring pain. Feeling that is sincere but sublimated, that is earnest yet restrained, is to be expressed. Avoidance of all artificialities, and concentration upon the musical beauty demanded, will help toward the right interpretation.

LUCIEN PATÉ
English version by
WILL EARHART

CÉSAR FRANCK

Original key

reap - 'er, reapt by death un - dy - ing, Sleeps gent - ly here.
mois - son - neu - se, mois - son - né - e Re - pose i - ci.

But on the tomb, in rest e - ter - nal,
Mais sur la tom - be qui vous cou - vre,

Where love doth lie,____ An eg - lan - tine for - ev - er ver - nal,
O mes a - mours!____ Une e - glan - ti - ne, qui s'en-tr'ou - vre,

Smiles to the sky.____ And 'neath the bend - ing branch - es__ kneel - ing,
Sou - rit tou - jours.____ Et sous le buis - son qui sur - plom - be,

Where lies my all,____ A mur - mured voice to me comes steal - ing:
Quand je re - viens,____ U - ne voix me dit sous la__ tom - be:

"I too, re - call."____
"Je me sou - viens."____

Leave Me In Sorrow
Lascia ch'io pianga from "Rinaldo"

Handel's opera Rinaldo, composed in 1711 in two weeks' time, was a notable work in a day when opera had first become a popular form of entertainment. As all such contemporary works, it has long passed from the stage, but remains in memory because of the rare beauty of the excerpt here given. Handel himself showed favor for this melody, for it first appears as a saraband in an opera that he composed seven years earlier. The stately tread of the saraband seems yet to control and give dignity to the passionate musings now reflected in the aria. The original recitative was for soprano and alto. The one here given, of unknown origin, was that used by the celebrated Henrietta Sontag (1804-1854).

English version by
WILL EARHART

G. F. HANDEL

Original key – F

Poco meno lento

O tears as - suag-ing pain's bit - ter rag-ing, From my great tor - ment in
Il duo-lo in-fran-ga que-ste ri-tor-te Dei miei mar - ti - ri, sol

pi - ty free me. From my great tor-ment, O set me free!
per pie - tà, Dei miei mar - ti - ri, sol per pie - tà.

Tempo primo

Leave me in sor-row that knows no mor-row; Deep is my
La - scia ch'io pian-ga mia cru - da sor - te, E che so -

The Cradles
Les Berceaux

Fauré's compositions in larger forms are not as widely current in America as in his native France, but many of his songs are favorably known here. *The Cradles* is one of a score of these that might further enrich the American repertory. It reveals the composer's power to create a distinctive mood or atmosphere, and discloses also his clearly defined melodic originality. The influence of the text upon the music is extremely powerful, leading at times to an almost point to point correspondence; but a sustained melodic sweep is nevertheless a salient feature of the composition to which the singer will need to pay due regard.

SULLY PRUDHOMME
English version by
WILL EARHART

GABRIEL FAURÉ

Original key— C minor

dream - ing, un-mind - ful of cra - - dles small,
pren - nent pas gar - - de aux ____ ber - ceaux,

Rocked by hands of wom - en a-pray - - ing. ____
Que la main des fem - mes ba - lan - - ce. ____

Soon must come the day of fare - well, ____
Mais vien - dra le jour des a - dieux, ____

Yet in that day___ the ves- -sels tall,___
Et ce jour là___ les grands___ vais- seaux,___

Fly- ing from port that fades a- way,___
Fuy- ant le port qui di- mi- nu- -e___

Feel their great frames held 'neath the sway___ Of
Sen- tent leur mas- -se re- te- nu- e Par

58

Maiden Tell Me

The naïve romance told in this little song must glow with the happiness of the expected lover's visit. The color of the voice of the curious questioner in the first stanza should be entirely different from that of the maiden who responds in the second and third verses. Even great singers often have difficulty finding just that intimate naïveté needed for a simple folk song, the difficulty of assuming the unassuming, so to speak. Understanding, simplicity and candor, rather than artifice, are needed.

English version by
FRANK LA FORGE

CZECHOSLOVAKIAN FOLKSONG
Arranged by
FRANK LA FORGE

Allegretto scherzando

1. Maid - en tell me, maid - en tell me! What art thou weav - ing, what art thou weav - ing In the morn - ing dew?
2. 'Tis a wreath that I am weav - ing Just a wreath of leaves and myr - tle And a crim - son rose.
3. 'Tis for him who loves me dear - ly Sun - day morn - ing he'll be com - ing Oh I love him so.

Farewell
Adieu!

This was originally in French and probably not the composition of Schubert. In the lyric prelude the sixteenth notes must receive their full value. This is not a song for display of broad dynamic effects but a quiet, intimate song of farewell. In songs of this nature it is important that the breath be taken very quietly and through the nostrils where time permits. Many otherwise beautiful renditions have been marred by too little thought of this important detail.

English version by
FRANK LA FORGE

FRANZ SCHUBERT (?)
(1797-1828)

Andante (*Moderately*)

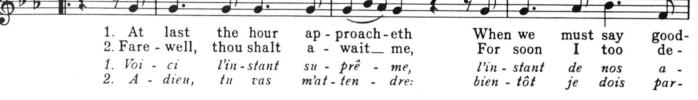

1. At last the hour ap - proach - eth When we must say good-
2. Fare - well, thou shalt a - wait me, For soon I too de-
1. *Voi - ci l'in - stant su - prê - me, l'in - stant de nos a-*
2. *A - dieu, tu vas m'at - ten - dre: bien - tôt je dois par-*

bye, O thou, my own be - lov - ed, Art called to go on
part. Thy mem - o - ry I'll cher - ish For - ev - er in my
dieux! Ô toi! seul bien que j'ai - me! sans moi re - tourne aux
tir. Mon cœur fi - dè - le et ten - dre te garde un sou - ve-

Original key

The Lotus Flower
Die Lotosblume

A phrase of a song has two main aspects, the musical and the literary. Before distorting the musical phrase in order to bring certain words together which should follow each other closely, be sure that by so doing you are not making the greater error of ruining the musical phrase. Such an instance occurs in this masterpiece, in the German text, where unwise singers sometimes connect the words "angstigt" and "sich" in spite of the rest which Schumann put between these words. The accompaniment should be played with great relaxation. Bringing out the upper C on the sixth count in the left hand of the twenty-fourth measure, and the F, A, D, and C following in the twenty-fifth measure, outlines a charming imitative figure.

HEINRICH HEINE
English version by
FRANK LA FORGE

ROBERT SCHUMANN, Op. 25, No. 7
(1810-1856)

moon, he is___ her lov - er,   He wak - ens her with his em -
Mond, der ist___ ihr Buh - le,   er weckt sie mit sei - nem

brace   And she   to him___ un - veil - eth   Her
Licht,   und ihm ent - schlei - ert siè freund - lich   ihr

pure_ and love - ly face.   She   glows   and blooms   and
from - mes Blu - men - ge - sicht.   Sie blüht   und glüht   und

The Song Of The Drummer
La Chanson du Tambourineur

Crisp in rhythm, precise in tempo, infectiously gay in melody, realistic in text, this song represents the salient characteristics of many French folksongs. But French nicety and lightness of touch are also reflected in the song, and any transgression by the singer in the direction of heavy pleasantry is consequently likely to spoil its charm.

English version by
WILL EARHART

OLD FRENCH SONG
XVIII Century
Accompaniment by
WILL EARHART

la_____ My roll-ing drum as well.
la_____ To serve my king, Loo-ee.
la_____ They'd serve him bet-ter far.　　　bold.
la_____ *Mon tam-bour-in aus-si.*
la_____ *Ser - vir le roi Lou-is.*
la_____ *Il se - rait mieux ser-vi.*　　　- si.

4	4
O then he'd capture cities,	*Il gagnerait des villes,*
la tzimm, la tzimm, la tzimm, la la,	*la tzimm, la tzimm, la tzimm, la la,*
O then he'd capture cities,	*Il gagnerait des villes,*
la tzimm, la tzimm, la la,	*la tzimm, la tzimm, la la,*
And castles big as well.	*Et des châteaux aussi.*

5	5
He'd marry off his daughters,	*Il marierait ses filles,*
la tzimm, la tzimm, la tzimm, la la,	*la tzimm, la tzimm, la tzimm, la la,*
He'd marry off his daughters,	*Il marierait ses filles,*
la tzimm, la tzimm, la la,	*la tzimm, la tzimm, la la,*
In bargain-matches rare.	*A de fort bons partis.*

6	6
Long live my valiant captain,	*Vive mon capitaine,*
la tzimm, la tzimm, la tzimm, la la,	*la tzimm, la tzimm, la tzimm, la la,*
Long live my valiant captain,	*Vive mon capitaine,*
la tzimm, la tzimm, la la,	*la tzimm, la tzimm, la la,*
And my lieutenant bold.	*Mon lieutenant aussi.*

For Music
Für Musik

The fragile beauty of this little gem must not be disturbed by any irregularity of rhythm. The final note of the first two verses is to be sustained with a supported relaxation which alone can give the floating tone required. The climax broadens in tempo but the last phrase returns to strict time as it fades away. The accompanist should not over-accent the notes which are identical with the vocal line but should allow the voice to predominate.

E. GEIBEL
English version by
FRANK LA FORGE

ROBERT FRANZ, Op. 10, No. 1
(1815-1887)

Innig (Andante molto sostenuto) *With fervor, well sustained*

Now the shad-ows fall-ing, Stars are all a-light;___
Nun die Schat-ten dun - keln, Stern an Stern er - wacht,___

What a breath of long - ing Floods the air___ to - night!___
welch ein Hauch der Sehn - sucht flu - tet durch___ die Nacht!___

Through the dream-land o - cean Rest-less floats my bark,___
Durch das Meer der Träu - me steu-ert oh - ne Ruh',___

Original key

Sleep, Little Angel
Hajej, můj andílku

Although little known in America, this lullaby is of rarest beauty and charm. Its flowing, undulant melody and somnolent cadences express the mood of the cradle song to perfection.

A small tone with the pervasive quality of the French Horn, rather than the pointed quality of the oboe, will best carry the echoing melody to the audience. It floats above a steadfast tonic bass that almost becomes a pastoral organ-point; and it is important that the accompanist give full value to this characteristic.

English version by
WILL EARHART

BOHEMIAN FOLKSONG

Sleep, lit - tle_ an - gel, now hush thee in sleep; Moth - er will rock thee and watch o'er thee keep.
Sleep, dear - est_ treas - ure, now hush thee in sleep; Close lit - tle eye - lids in dream-slum - ber deep.

Sleep, lit - tle_ an - gel, now hush thee in sleep;
Sleep, dear - est_ treas - ure, now hush thee in sleep;

Now Suffer Me, Fair Maiden
Erlaube mir, fein's Mädchen

The tenderness and delicate grace of this song are best brought out by refinement of tone and by a diction that must be crystal clear, but never declamatory. A cantilena, in short, punctuated rhythmically by consonants, but not destroyed by them, should be sought. The most emphasis, of course, attends the *crescendo* in the third phrase.

No folksongs have had more ideal arrangement than that accorded by Brahms to his German folk-songs. His accompaniments seem to carry these natural flowers of song to a goal that they dimly sought but could not reach. In the thirteenth and fourteenth measures of the song below, for instance, his exquisite harmonies make articulate a beauty that otherwise must have remained mute.

English version by
WILL EARHART

GERMAN FOLKSONG
Arranged by Johannes Brahms
(1833-1897)

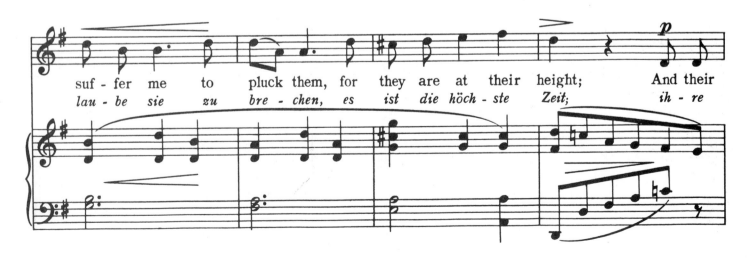

fresh-ness, their beau-ty, have fill'd me with de-light.
Schön-heit, ihr' Ju-gend hat mir mein Herz er-freut.

O
O

maid-en, O maid-en, you thrice love-ly child, Who now with the fan-cy your
Mäd-chen, O Mäd-chen, du ein-sa-mes Kind, wer hat den Ge-dan-ken in's

heart has be-guil'd That I shall the gar-den the ros-es not see: To my
Herz dir ge-zinnt, dass ich soll den Gar-ten, die Ro-sen nicht sehn; du ge-

eyes you are pleas-ing; so far I a-gree.
fällst mei-nen Au-gen dass muss ich ge-stehn.

In Evening's Glow
Im Abendrot

The impression of the glory of a sunset upon the poet and the composer has perpetuated for humanity this mood of gratitude to the Creator. A reverent nobility of interpretation, devoid of superficiality, is required.

C. LAPPE
English version by
FRANK LA FORGE

FRANZ SCHUBERT
(1797-1828)

O, how fair thy beau - teous world Fa - ther, when thy sun - light
O, wie schön ist dei - ne Welt, Va - ter, wenn sie gold - en

gold - en beams, And thy glance rests here — be - low.
strah - let! wenn dein Glanz her - nie - der fällt,

Original key

To Part, Ah Grief Unending
Ach Gott, wie weh tut Scheiden

The passionate intensity of this song can be projected by energy of enunciation (amounting at times to a greater or slighter *sforzando*) by somewhat abrupt contrasts in power between phrase and phrase, and in free and sensitive departures from an even-flowing tempo. Dramatic quality also brings the words of a song into a position of greater importance, and the expression must be constantly moulded to suit their meaning. The ending of the first stanza, for instance, needs simplicity, wistfulness, almost self-pity; the same melody in the second stanza must have the quality of great pathos, and this will require postponement of the *diminuendo* and somewhat more emphasis on single notes. This same ending must be still more greatly modified in the last stanza — largely, perhaps, by a strong *ritardando* — or there will be almost danger of anti-climax.

English version by
WILL EARHART

GERMAN FOLKSONG
Arranged by Johannes Brahms
(1833-1897)

Moved, with passionate feeling

1. To part, ah grief un - end - ing! The pain has wrung my heart. O'er
2. A gar - den I cre - at - ed of fern and vio - let blue; To
1. Ach Gott, wie weh tut Schei - den, hat mir mein Herz ver - wund't, so
2. Hatt' mir ein Gärt - lein bau - et, von Veil und grü - nem Klee, ist

waste of moor - land wend - ing, I bear my cross a - part. Too
ear - ly blight 'twas fat - ed and I am left the rue. Yes
trab' ich üb'r die Hai - den und traur' zu al - ler Stund. Der
mir zu früh er - fro - ren, tut mei - nem Her - zen weh. Ist

When Love Is Kind

An old English song which lends variety to a program and which is, at the same time, vocally grateful.

THOMAS MOORE

ANONYMOUS

When Love is kind, cheer-ful and free, Love's sure to find wel-come from me.
If Love can sigh for one a - lone, Well pleas'd am I to be that one.

But when love brings heart-ache and pang, Tears and such things, Love may go hang.
But should I see Love giv'n to rove To two or three, then good-bye Love.

The Sandman

This little sprite has inspired many composers. He sprinkles sand on the eyes of children to make them sleep, and is an especially beloved figure in German legendary lore. This song should be sung in the manner of a lullaby. The third verse is effective in slow movement and sung pianissimo.

English version by
FRANK LA FORGE

GERMAN FOLKSONG
From the Lower Rhine
Arranged by
FRANK LA FORGE

1. The flow'r - ets have been sleep - ing Long since in moon - light fair. Their heads are gent - ly nod - ding On stems in si - lence there.
2. The lit - tle birds were sing - ing So sweet - ly in the sun, But now they all are nest - ing And dream - ing ev - 'ry one.
3. The sand - man comes on tip - toe And views each ti - ny head, To find per - chance a tru - ant Who had not gone to bed.

Return To The Mountain Home
Auf der Reise zur Heimat

The essential human quality of folksong pervades the words and the greater part of the melody of this song, and only in the accompaniment, especially in the fifth and sixth phrases, do we feel the composer becoming preoccupied with sheer compositional tone-weavings.

The mood is one of deep musing, of complete absorption. What is in the mind of the dreamer lives more vividly than that which is before his eyes. If the singer addresses the song too pointedly to his hearers, that effect of inner communion will be lost. Only under this interpretation too, will the dynamic restraint which the singer will feel the composer has imposed upon him appear appropriate. When the dynamic climax does come—in the fourth measure from the end—it is still unconscious of itself, though full-throated and sweeping.

A.O. VINJE
English version by
WILL EARHART

EDVARD GRIEG, Op. 33, No. 9
(1843-1907)

Snowbells
Schneeglökchen

To be sung with unaffected simplicity. The first verse should be sung in a simple narrative tone, but, in the second verse from "with snowbells ringing hark the message," a note of joyful anticipation must color the tone. The right hand part of the accompaniment is to be played with a light and resonant touch, carrying out the suggestion of little bells.

FRIEDRICH RÜCKERT
English version by
FRANK LA FORGE

ROBERT SCHUMANN, Op. 79, No. 27
(1810-1856)

The snow that yes-ter-day was fall - ing
Der Schnee, der ges-tern noch in Flöck-chen

From heav'n a - bove, Hangs all__ melt-ed now as snow-bells
vom Him - mel fiel, hängt nun ge - ron - nen heut' als Glöck-chen

On ten - der stems. The snow-bell's ring-ing, hark the mes-sage,
am zar - ten Stiel. Schnee-glöck-chen läu-tet; was be - deu-tet's

Original key – D

With A Water Lily
Mit einer Wasserlilie

Usually published for soprano a tone lower. The editor finds this tonality too low for soprano and too high for contralto. The dramatic section expressing anxiety sets off well the more tranquil parts, and must be projected with adequate feeling.

HENRIK IBSEN
English version by
FRANK LA FORGE

EDVARD GRIEG, Op. 25, No. 4
(1843-1907)

See,____ Ma - ri - a, what I'm bring - ing! Lil - ies white from wa - ter spring - ing. On the riv - er____ calm - ly____ float - ing

Sieh,____ Ma - ri - a, was ich brin - ge: Blu - me mit der wei-ssen Schwin - ge, auf des Stro - mes stil - len Wo - gen

Verdant Meadows
Verdi Prati
(From "Alcina" 1735)

To be a worthy singer of Handel is to have great nobility of style, breath control, and an appreciation of real *bel canto*. Handel's stay in Italy gave his genius still another facet in combining the Italian vocal style with the German grandeur and power.

In many of the works of the early Italian composers an agility is required which dramatic singers of today find difficulty in executing. At the time these were written all voices, whether coloratura or dramatic, were expected to be capable of this agility.

English version by
FRANK LA FORGE

G.F. HÄNDEL
(1685-1759)

Larghetto *(Slowly)*

Ver - dant mead-ows, woods be-
Ver - di pra - ti e sel - ve a -

lov - ed; Soon_ will fade thy beau-ty rare. Love-ly flow'rs,
me - ne, per - de - re - te la__ bel - tà, Va - ghe fior,

flow - ing riv - ers, All thy beau-ty, all thy beau - ty
cor - ren - ti ri - vi, la va - ghez - za, la bel - lez - za

Original key— E

94

All thy charms will come a - gain Ver - dant
tut - to in voi ri - tor - ne - rà. Ver - di

mead - ows, woods be - lov - ed Soon will fade thy
pra - ti e sel - ve a - me - ne, per - de - re - te

beau - ty rare, Soon will fade thy beau - ty rare.
la bel - tà, per - de - re - te la bel - tà.

The Rose Complains
Es hat die Rose sich beklagt

Robert Franz was one of the greatest but lesser known of the German song composers, ranking easily with Schubert, Schumann and Brahms. His real name was Knauth. He wrote over three hundred and fifty songs;—miniatures of the greatest beauty. His genius was recognized by Liszt and others of his day, who helped him financially. In more recent times Lilli Lehmann gave many recitals consisting entirely of his songs, thus familiarizing the concert world with their worth.

Although small in form, these songs require an amazing breath support to negotiate the long phrases. "The Rose Complains" is no exception and the final phrase of each verse should be sung in one breath.

MIRZA-SCHAFFY
English version by
FRANK LA FORGE

ROBERT FRANZ, Op. 42, No. 5
(1815-1892)

Night and Dreams
Nacht und Träume

In *Night and Dreams,* Schubert again summons all the components of a mood with the prescience and infallibility of a seer. It is an uncommon mood in music. The spirit is caught up in glowing, moonlit space, and clings to its hour of wonder.

Fragile as is the mood, the manner of singing by which it may be projected is perhaps not so difficult. Ample breath, easily taken and expansively retained, and a stream of pure, unlabored tone that flows without breaking into ripples over underlying consonants, are requisites for the more exacting first and last parts. The middle part—the beginning of the second section—has, of course, more substantial and earthly quality.

MATTHÄUS von COLLIN
English version by
WILL EARHART

FRANZ SCHUBERT Op. 43, No. 2
(1797-1828)

There's Weeping In My Heart
(Il pleure dans mon coeur)

Although Debussy was a French composer, his teacher, Ernest Guiraud, was born in New Orleans, Louisiana, of French parentage. Guiraud was the only one who recognized the genius of Debussy and encouraged him in his modernistic ideas. This song is one of the finest examples of Debussy's work.

ACHILLE-CLAUDE DEBUSSY
(1862-1918)

Modérément animé *(triste et monotone)*

There's weep - - ing in my
Il pleu - - re dans mon -

heart as it rains on the town
coeur Comme il pleut sur la vil - - le

Whence this lan - guor which steals soft - ly
Quelle est cet - te lan - gueur Qui pé -

in ─ ─ to my heart
nè ─ ─ tre mon coeur

O gen - tle sound of the rain On the ground and the
O bruit doux de la plui - e Par terre et sur les

roofs!
toits!

For a heart that is griev - ing O the
Pour un coeur qui s'en - nui - e O le

song of the rain! This
bruit de la pluie! Il

griev - ing with - out cause In this
pleu - re sans rai - son Dans ce

heart which is pin - ing
coeur qui s'é - coeu - re

How?   no de-cep-tion here   this grief   is with-out
Quoi!   *nul-le tra - hi - son?*   *Ce deuil*   *est sans rai-*

cause
son

Tempo I

Yes   'tis   the   keen - est   of   pain   that   one
C'est   *bien*   *la*   *pi - re*   *pei - ne De*   *ne*

ne'er   may   know   why   with-out   lov - ing   or
sa - voir   *pour - quoi,*   *sans a - mour et*   *sans*

Longing For Spring

This little song was written in the year of Mozart's death and became immensely popular in Germany as a child's song. The opening phrase "Come lovely May and make the forests green again" should be sung in one breath, but in the second verse one should breathe after the word "singing." The indication "joyfully" would suggest, in this case, "allegretto" but too fast a tempo is not advisable for this gentle lyric.

CHR. A. OVERBECK
English version by
FRANK LA FORGE

W. A. MOZART
(1756-1791)

Original key

rit.

how I love___ to gath - er them, to gath - er them___ once
now the snow___ is on the ground and we___ must stay___ in -

a tempo

more. And tread the for - est path - ways as
side. Come love - ly May with flow - - ers, we'll

we___ have done___ be - fore.
roam___ the mead - ows wide.

The Kiss
Der Kuss

This song is possibly more suitable for a man, but it has been in the repertoire of many of the greatest women singers. If one were to eliminate from the repertoires of women singers all the songs written for men and vice versa, the result would be too far reaching to be practical. The quaint humor which Beethoven expresses in this music is a fine example of his masterly handling of texts.

English version by
FRANK LA FORGE

L. van BEETHOVEN
(1770-1827)

Night
Die Nacht

This song, from Opus 10, *Acht Gedichte* (Eight Poems), is one of Strauss' earlier compositions. A change which took place in his style and, indeed, in his whole musical creed, was only forecast some years later, in his Opus 16, *Aus Italien*, a fantasia for orchestra. That change consisted in a movement away from the classical tradition and into the marked expressivist, romantic-realistic style in which his later and greater works are cast. Nevertheless, *Die Nacht*, although of comparative simplicity, is a most effective song. The transition from the mood of evening — of gathering darkness — to the agitated outburst, near the close, followed by an almost shuddering subsidence, is masterfully managed by the composer. The song is, moreover, admirably adapted both to the voice and to the types of feeling which the singer experiences. Mme Sembrich always programmed "Die Nacht" —— "Morgen" together and sang these songs without pausing between. This arrangement was most artistic and effective.

HERM. v. GILM
English version by
WILL EARHART

RICHARD STRAUSS, Op. 10, No. 3
(1864-1949)

113

To Friendship
An die Freundschaft

The poetic fervor and individual dramatic character with which Schubert invested every song he wrote **drew** preference away, for a time, from the less vivid pages of Haydn and Mozart. Now that Schubert's and still later veins of expression have become familiar to us, our taste is rightly expanding to include many kinds of excellence. In this song we should be prepared to accept classical restraint in place of emotional release, and beauty of tone and dignity of phrasing in place of strong dramatic delineation. For establishing good vocal foundations such exchange of values may prove to be advantageous.

English version by
WILL EARHART

JOSEPH HAYDN

Original key—G

A Very Ordinary Story
Eine sehr gewöhnliche Geschichte

Haydn the pious, Haydn the genial, could also become Haydn the wag, with a turn for almost a boisterous humor. So much is evident in this song, not only by reason of Haydn's choice of words, but in his obvious delight in piling rushing sixteenth notes into his accompaniment to suggest the impetuosity of Philint's knocking.

The song will require clean and clear articulation, but must not become non-tonal chattering. To preserve the sense of a tonal line, as it would be were an organ to play the melody *staccato,* and yet to articulate well and rapidly, will be an excellent study for the singer, and will make the song a joyous experience for the hearer.

CHRISTIAN FELIX WEISSE
English version by
WILL EARHART

JOSEPH HAYDN
(1732-1809)

3. He sadly turns and would be gone,
When quick he hears the latchet drawn,
When quick he hears the latchet drawn,
the latchet drawn, the latchet drawn.
‖:He hears: "Well, then, a moment stay,
But go you soon away." :‖

4. The prying neighors all about
Were keeping watch till he came out,
In silent indignation they
Did loudly pound upon the door,
"Now where's Philint? He should be home.
The hour is striking four."
"Why he went home at nine o'clock,
But he went by another door."

3. *Bekümmert will er wieder gehn,*
da hört er schnell den Schlüssel drehn,
da hört er schnell den Schlüssel drehn,
den Schlüssel drehn, den Schlüssel drehn.
‖: *Er hört: „Auf einen Augenblick,*
doch geh auch gleich zurück!" :‖

4. *Die Nachbarn plagt die Neugier sehr;*
sie warteten der Wiederkehr,
sie warteten der Wiederkehr,
der Wiederkehr, der Wiederkehr.
‖: *Er kam auch, doch erst morgens früh.*
Ei, ei, wie lachten sie! :‖

To The Beloved
Ah die Geliebte

Beethoven made two settings of this poem. The second, composed possibly in 1812 but not published until 1840, is the one here used. Beethoven's songs, as indeed all his music, are weighted with a deeper emotional tone than the songs of Haydn and Mozart, but the possibility of concentrating a wide glimpse of life into the small limits of an art-song, as Schubert did it, had not yet been revealed. Breadth of expression and care for purely musical values must accordingly be preserved in singing his songs.

English version by
WILL EARHART

L. van BEETHOVEN

Andantino, un poco agitato *(Moderately, but with emotion)*

O that I might the tear drop show-ing In thy dear eye with
O dass ich dir vom stil - len Au - ge in sei - nem lie - be-

lus - ter bright, From dew - y cheek where now___ 'tis flow-ing,
vol - len Schein die Trä - ne von der Wan - ge sau - ge,

Drink, ere the earth shall quaff its light!
eh' sie die Er - de trin - ket ein!

Original key

In The Country
Die Landlust

Freshness and charm of inspiration are outstanding characteristics of Haydn's works. This mood reflects the joy of communing with Nature and exhales relaxation and release from care. It might be well to count two to a measure with strong accents on the first beat. The first part of the second verse should be sung softer than the first verse to better illustrate the words. If phrases one and two, also three and four, are sung as one, gasping for breath will be avoided and smoothness contributed to the rendition. The three final measures may be used as an introduction.

English version by
FRANK LA FORGE

JOSEPH HAYDN
(1732-1809)

1. A - way_ from care_ and sor - row, I glad - ly greet the mor - row, When I_ through-out the night,_ Have slept till morn - ing light. With free-dom in_ my heart,_ With

2. I rest_ me here_ and lis - ten, And watch the brook - let flow_ From out_ the rocks and bush - es, Where moss and ferns do grow. I hear so far_ a - bove me, I

1. Ent - fernt_ von Gram und Sor - gen, er - wach' ich je - den Mor - gen, wenn ich_ vor - her die Nacht_ sanft schlumm-ernd hin - ge - bracht. Die Frei - heit in_ dem Her - zen, die

2. Hier ruh' ich und_ er - gö - tze mich an_ des Bach's Ge - schwä - tze, der halb_ im Busch ver - hüllt,_ leis' aus dem Fel - sen quillt; hör' sie_ in blau - en Lüf - ten, hör'

Original key

Come, Sweet Death

Komm, süsser Tod

This song is from Schemelli's song collection. The genius of Bach shines forth in these few lines as brightly as in his greatest works. It should be sung with religious fervor and humility, and in the style of a choral, allowing ample time for breathing.

English version by
FRANK LA FORGE

JOHANN SEBASTIAN BACH
(1685-1750)

1. Come, come sweet death, Come blessed rest! Come and give me peace. Of this life I'm wear-y, Oh come I wait for thee, come soon and lead me. Ah, close my wear-y eyes, Come bless-ed rest!

2. Come, come sweet death, Come blessed rest! I would now see Je-sus and with the an-gels will I stand, Ah, yes it is fin-ished I bid the world good-night. I close my wear-y eyes, Come bless-ed rest!

1. Komm, sü-sser Tod, komm, sel'-ge Ruh'! komm, füh-re mich in Frie-de, weil ich der Welt bin mü-de, ach, komm, ich wart' auf dich, füh-re mich, drück' mir die Au-gen zu. Komm, sel'-ge Ruh'!

2. Komm, sü-sser Tod, komm, sel'-ge Ruh'! Ich will nun Je-sum se-hen und bei den En-geln ste-hen. Es ist nun-mehr voll-bracht, drum, Welt, zu gu-ter Nacht! mein' Au-gen sind schon zu. Komm, sel'-ge Ruh'!

Tomorrow
Morgen

The *Vier Lieder* (Four Songs) that constitute Strauss' Opus 27 have all won the affection of singers, but none more than *Morgen*. The lovely and noble mood and the masterly composition—possible only to a profoundly gifted composer—make the song an outstanding one, even in the company of the world's greatest songs.

Technically, however, the song is not beyond the singer of modest accomplishment. Musical intelligence and artistic feeling are more needed, indeed, than advanced vocal capabilities. The singer should observe that the long and lovely prelude is hauntingly repeated to form the accompaniment to the voice. The singing will be most effective if it enters unobtrusively over this instrumental revery, and continues clearly and yet in perfect accord with its instrumental companion. Pure tone, perfect and unwavering intonation, an un-broken legato, and no large or abrupt dynamic changes, are further essentials.

JOHN HENRY MACKAY
English version by
WILL EARHART

RICHARD STRAUSS, Op. 27, No. 4
(1864-1949)

molto tranquillo

To-mor-row will the sun a - gain___ be shin - ing, And in the
Und mor-gen wird die Son-ne wie - der schei - nen und auf dem

road - way that my feet shall cap - ture Shall we, the hap - py ones,
We - ge, den ich ge - hen wer - de, wird uns, die Glück - li-chen,

our hands en - twin - - ing, Be join-ed in a world of sun - breath-ing
sie wie - der ei - - nen in-mit-ten die-ser son - nen-at - men-den

rap - ture. And toward a strand where wide___ waves blue are
Er - de und zu dem Strand, dem wei - - ten, wo-gen-

The Rose And The Lily
Die Rose, die Lilie, die Taube

Ordinarily Schumann entrusts to the piano accompaniments of his songs certain shades of poetic quality that the voice and text alone can not, he seems to feel, dilate upon, even if they can rightly express. It is a practice that Wagner carried to the furthest limits: and it contrasts sharply with the style of the old Italian masters of *bel canto,* in which long-flowing melodic phrases hold substantially the whole of the composer's intention.

But in *The Rose and the Lily*—one of *Dichterliebe,* a group of sixteen songs, all on texts by Heinrich Heine —we have a Schumann song of another type. In it the composer slips the leash from an animated melody that wings at once into unhesitating flight. No poetic musings and colorings are needed for such a forthright melody, and Schumann here, as in other songs of the kind, provides a simple, although always appropriate and effective, chord accompaniment. Such a song is grateful to the singer because it releases him from complex musical considerations and enables him to concentrate wholly on his melodic line. Nevertheless the present song will not be easy, since the demands for facile enunciation, skillful breath control, and tonal steadiness, are all exacting.

HEINRICH HEINE
English version by
WILL EARHART

ROBERT SCHUMANN, Op. 48, No. 3
(1810-1856)

The rose and the li - ly, the dove, sun a - gleam - ing, I
Die Ro - se, die Li - lie, die Tau - be, die Son - ne, die

once loved them dear - ly in rap - tured dream - ing; I
liebt ich einst al - le in Lie - bes - won - ne. Ich

love them no more; a - lone do I love her, The fair one, the rare one, O
lieb' sie nicht mehr, ich lie - be al - lei - ne die Klei - ne, die Fei - ne, die

Dance Song

In the old villages of Czechoslovakia very large tile stoves occupy about a fourth of the one room which constitutes a peasant's home. The occupants not only heat and bake with these stoves, but sleep on them as well. This song should be sung with dash and abandon. It makes its demands on temperament and style rather than on range of voice. The accents on the first count of the 7th and 8th measures, as in all similar ones, are important.

English version by
FRANK LA FORGE

CZECHOSLOVAKIAN FOLKSONG
Arranged by
FRANK LA FORGE